Let
Me Say
That Again

Let Me Say That Again

MAXIMS FOR SPIRITUAL LIVING

Maxie Dunnam

UPPER
ROOM BOOKS
NASHVILLE

Cover Design: Bruce Gore
Interior Design: Nancy Cole and Bruce Gore
First Printing: February 1996 (7)
Library of Congress Catalog Number: 95-62142
ISBN: 0-8358-0769-X

Printed in the United States of America

Introduction

EVERY PUBLIC SPEAKER develops a unique style. Rate of speech, intonation, sentence structure, theme development, introductions, conclusions, use of humor, and many other elements form the style of every speaker. Students study effective communicators and seek to learn from them.

Much of the development of a speaking style is conscious, although some is unconscious. Somewhere along the way, unconsciously, in my preaching, I developed a technique of emphasis and repetition. When I make a primary point in a sermon—a core idea, truth, an affirmation—before I explain further, I will say, "Let me say that again." Then I will deliberately repeat my statement to lodge it solidly in the minds and hearts of the listeners. While developing a sermon, I may do this five or six times. I then often close the worship service with a benediction that restates these central affirmations. My intention is to make these succinct, gripping statements so available to the mind and memory of the hearers that they will be able to have specific thoughts for reflection in the days following.

Members of my congregation would often tease me about my style. In group conversation, someone would say slyly, "Let me say that again." Some members even began to refer to my statements as "Maxie's maxims." That's what this book is: a collection of thoughts I want to say again and again.

The dictionary defines a maxim as "a brief statement of a general principle, truth or rule of conduct." It is something like a proverb, a pithy saying that condenses wisdom, a few words that express the essence of an idea, a notion, a truth, a guide for living.

The maxims in this volume have come primarily from unpublished sermons and two published works: Volumes One and Two of *Perceptions* (Bristol House). These maxims are my effort to congeal truth into bite-sized expressions. It is the nature of truth that gets a "yes" response that denotes anyone could have made the statement. And so it is with these expressions.

If you put these maxims into practice, you will change. Thus, don't just sit down and read this book from beginning to end. Open it wherever you will and read until you come to a maxim you need to latch on to. Live with it, apply it, share it. Keep the book in a place where it is readily accessible. Pick it up at random moments and ponder some relevant instruction for your life. An alternative idea is to center daily on one of these maxims. Let it be the life principle that you work on for the day.

I commend these maxims to you because they have changed and enriched my life. Read these truths, ponder them, memorize them, recast them in your own words, make them your own, and share them with a friend.

$\mathcal{M}$ost of us prefer
the hell of a predictable situation
rather than risk the joy
of an unpredictable one.

*B*eing a Christian means
we never have to be alone again.

---

*W*e commit suicide on the
installment plan when we
harbor resentment, cultivate self-pity,
nourish shame, and refuse to forgive.

*T*here is only one way
the puzzle of life will fit together,
and that's God's way.

———————

*T*o be loved in general will never
meet the deepest needs of our lives.
We must be loved in particular.

*S*ometimes we have to step into the sea
before the waters will be parted.

———

*T*here are so many issues in life
that would be settled,
that would not drain us of the
energy involved in decision making,
if we would settle once and for all
who we are and whose we are.

*T*he presence of God in Jesus Christ is
not to be experienced only occasionally.
The indwelling Christ is to become
the shaping power of our lives.

*D*oing beats talking every time.

———

*T*he need to control is an expression
of a distorted need for security.

We must be careful what we bury in our heart. To bury something does not mean it is dead. It may simply mean we have buried something alive that will devour and destroy us from within.

*T*o love is to be vulnerable.
If you want to be safe
from pain, don't love.

---

*T*he circumstances of life are
never as important as our attitudes
toward those circumstances.

What we have does not determine whether we have the kingdom.

To trust Christ is not to have a life free of trials and temptations, but to have the confidence that the "one who is in you is greater than the one who is in the world."

We have become so
heavenly minded that we are
no earthly good.

*W*e are committing an
unspeakable crime against ourselves
when we drown ourselves
in negative thinking.

*I*f we are not willing to be patient with people and stick with them until they're free to share their inner struggle with us, we can at least not add to their burden by judging them.

*T*he double-minded person
becomes a walking civil war in which
trusting and distrusting God
wage a continual battle.

When we say a solid "yes" to God,
we are given discernment as to
what we should say "no" to
and the power to say it.
And then our "no" to those things
becomes a "yes" to God.

*G*od never lets us down,
never lets us off,
and never lets us go!

*M*ost of us would be amazed by
how much more effective we would be
in our witnessing if we stopped talking
and began to listen.

When we dishonor the poor,
we dishonor God.

———

There are no favorites and no
strangers in the Lord's fellowship
of believers.

*R*epentance is more than just acknowledging our sin; it is also the deep desire to cease our sinful actions and be freed of our sinful attitudes and feelings.

When we love,
what hurts another hurts us;
what brings them sorrow
brings us tears.

*T*he person who is rich,
in the richest sense, is the one
who has learned to be content
in any circumstance.

*T*here are some things
God either cannot or will not do
until and unless people pray.

*P*rayer does something *in* us.
Prayer does something *for* us.
Prayer does something *through* us.

———

*T*here is never a road so long
that there's not a bend in it.

A Christian is
hopelessly in love with Jesus
and *helplessly* dependent upon him.

*T*here is hope for us,
even in our sin and failure,
as long as we are haunted by goodness.

———

*W*e should not let yesterday
rob us of tomorrow.

We easily deplete
our emotional energy
by needlessly anticipating
the bad which never comes.

———

Life is life by the choices we make.

*N*ever expect God to act
before we are willing.

———

*W*e will never realize
how important we are
until we realize and accept
how small we are.

*O*nly when we grow weary enough
of our present situation are we
likely to seek and risk change.

*B*oth work and free time
will control us until, and unless,
we control them.

———

*T*he more enslaved we are to Christ,
the freer we are.

*T*he secret of life is not
a change of jobs, a change of scenery,
or a change of circumstances,
but a change of heart.

———————

*G*iving to another is the greatest gift
we can give to ourselves.

*D*oing things right
is not nearly as important
as doing the right things.

*I*f we cannot afford to spend time
with God and alone with ourself,
we will remain poor forever.

*W*e must be careful about what
we desire. Getting what we want
can cause as much unhappiness
as not getting what we want.

———

*T*he reason we don't enjoy others
may be that we don't enjoy ourselves.

*B*ecause there are many reasons
to stay where we are
doesn't mean we should
close our mind to change.

———————

*F*orgiveness means more than pardon,
it means letting go.

*W*e can count on it:
What is good for the kingdom
of God will be good for us.
But it doesn't work the other way.

———

*T*he difference between being called
and being driven is whether we or
our job are calling the shots.

*B*e careful. It is easier to prefer
the hustle and bustle that diverts us
rather than the solitude that enables us
to discern who we really are.

---

*O*n the road of life
one of the most serious violations
is to ignore the signal
to stop, look, and listen.

*T*he measure of life is whether
you are fully used up when you die.

*T*he difference between our life as it is
and as we would like it to be
is primarily a matter of will.

---

*L*ove always means having to say,
"I'm sorry, forgive me."

*T*o win in the game of life,
we must substitute "next time"
for "if only."

———

*A*ddiction to success
makes us a slave.

We must make sure that
if we get to where we are going,
we will be where we want to be.

———————

We can't buy a fiddle today
and expect to give a concert
in Carnegie Hall tomorrow.

*T*he blame and shame of yesterday
will bury us
if we don't bury them.

*T*he best way to cure the
"poor me" disease is to do something
for someone else.

*T*he reason for a Christian's weakness
is the weakness of the Christian's faith.

We must pay attention to our fears.
When we are afraid, our heart is trying
to tell us something.

We must be careful
that we don't blame others
for what is wrong with us.

*R*esentment is a cancer
for which there is only one cure:
confession and forgiveness.

———

*F*ailure may be the first step
to something better.

*L*ife doesn't promise us anything,
except a chance.

———

*T*he peril of riches is that they tend to
bring us a false sense of security.

*W*e never see ourselves clearly
until we see ourselves
through the eyes of others.

———

*I*f we are worried about whether
what we are doing is right,
we should ask, "Would God see this
as an act of love and care?"

*B*ecause the road to hell is paved
with good intentions does not mean
that we cease from being intentional;
we must add will and commitment
to our intentions.

Give others the freedom
to be themselves,
and claim the same freedom
for yourself.

Surrender is not a sign of weakness;
it is the pathway of love and relationship,
especially the relationship of marriage
and our relationship to God.

*T*o build our life around
someone we love is limiting;
to include that one in building our life
is fulfilling.

We act our way into Christ likeness.
To be like Christ
we must act like Christ.

———————

When we discover the loving, gentle
side of ourselves, we will have power
we never dreamed of possessing.

*H*ope is never demanding,
always affirming.

———————

*T*here is no place
to hide from temptation.
The nature of temptation changes,
but the tempter is always looking
for the more opportune time.

*W*e don't keep secrets;
our secrets keep us.

———

*L*earning to let go is one of life's
most important lessons.

*T*he toughest battle you will ever fight
is between you and yourself.

———

I'm well along the path of becoming
when I am secure enough
to laugh at myself.

*B*e careful what you hide in your heart;
your tongue will find it and tell it.

———

*L*ife is neither good nor bad;
it includes both.

*T*o laugh at another is a painful blow;
to laugh with them
is a "yes" to their being.

———

*E*very life is a candle, but some lives
are torches that burn brightly
and provide light to be passed on
to other generations.

*R*esentment is unexpressed and
unresolved anger grown sour.
Nothing sweet can come from it.
In fact, it will sour your whole life.

———

*W*e must take good care of ourselves
in order to take good care of others.

When you listen to me you say to me,
"You are important; I value you."

———————

We may invite others to love us;
we cannot order them to do so.

*I*t is not likely that
we will be patient with others
unless we are patient with ourselves.

———

*A*re we paying attention
to what we fear losing most?

*T*here is a sense in which we become
as sick as the secrets we keep.

---

*R*epentance is the experience
that enables us to close the door
on yesterday.

*E*xpecting too much happiness
may blind us to the happiness
that is already ours.

———

*A*ccepting our faults
goes hand in hand
with affirming our virtues.

What we really love
tells the story of who we are.

—————

We grow the most when
we pay attention to
our mistakes and failures.

*I*t's more important to
pay attention to what people do
than to what they say.

———

*R*eleasing another
to go his or her own way
gives us the same freedom.

We may be converted to Christ
in the miracle of a moment,
but becoming a saint
is the task of a lifetime.

*T*rying to be perfect,
in terms of performance,
is the surest path to failure.

We must never think that we are going somewhere that Jesus has not been, that we are tempted in a way that Jesus was not tempted, that we are suffering in a way that Jesus could not understand.

*T*here is only one thing
more costly than caring,
and that is not caring.

———

*W*e know that all of us
are going to die. But do we live
as though we know it?

We trust God
for some things, sometimes;
we need to trust God
for all things, all the time.

As Christians we do not
emerge full blown; we grow.
And we grow by discipline.

*I*t's a lie

that how much we succeed
determines our worth;

that who we know is more important
than what we do;

that the end justifies the means;

that if we don't dominate,
we will be losers.

*I*t's a lie
that we must make our decisions
out of selfish interest because if we don't
care about ourselves no one else will;

that we must deny our failure and
hide our weakness in order to
maintain our image of strength;

that we must forget the future because
survival now is the name of the game;

that we must use whatever power we have
for our own sakes because that's what
power is for—to "feather our own nest."

*I*f God can wait,
if God can love and not manipulate,
then God can certainly give us the power
to resist the temptation to control
those we love.

*I*f we don't have love,
we are less than human.
If we are less than human,
we are less than God intended us to be.

———

*O*ther persons as channels of God's
love are essential for life's journey.

*T*he same light that exposes our sin
also cleanses us of it.

———

*S*ome persons are ruled as compulsively
by negative thoughts
as those who are ruled by more obvious
addictions such as drugs or sex.

*T*here is a place in God's heart
that only *I* can fill.

On the seventh day God rested from all the work which was done in creation. If we say we don't have time to rest, we are playing one-upmanship with God.

*W*e should not go looking for
something we think will make us happy
before we pay attention to
what we already have.

———

*L*ove is a decision. It is something
we do—an act of will
that gives itself unselfishly for the
good and enrichment of another.

*L*ife is too short to feel guilty.
If we want to get rid of our guilt,
we must stop doing what causes it.

———————

"*L*ord, make our words
sweet and tender today
for we may have to eat them tomorrow."

*F*ailure is not a word of cowards and fools. It is the word of heroes and wise folk who keep dreaming dreams though some dreams are never realized.

———

*L*aughter is healing. It takes our mind off ourself and relieves stress.

*H*ave you ever done anything so powerful in a demonstration of love and courage that it made a difference in someone else's life?

*I*f we keep our attention on the present,
the past won't haunt us;
nor will the future burden us with fear.

———

*T*oday we have the chance to live
as though what happened in the past
doesn't matter.

*T*he best way to get help
is to ask for it.

———————

*I*f we discover our choice is wrong,
we don't have to feel like a *wrong* person.
We can learn from our mistakes
without slinking into shame
or self-pity.

*N*o one feels loved by someone
who seeks to control them.

———

*T*o be a whole person,
and to overcome boredom,
two things are essential:
1) faith to live by and
2) a cause to live for.

*C*onsider this rule for life:
Cry if you must,
but laugh if you can.

*P*retending to be perfect
prevents us from being real.

*T*he problem with most of us is that
we want to get to the promised land
without going through the wilderness.

We make the decision as to whether
the events of our life will serve as
stepping stones or stumbling blocks.

*I*f we are overly concerned about our image—if we are preoccupied with the impression we are making on other people—the chances are that we are not certain of our own identity.

*T*he best way to say no to something
is to say yes to its counterpart.
The best way to get rid of a bad habit
is to replace it with a good one.

*B*efore this day ends do two things:

1) Tell a person
you have not told recently
that you love them.

2) For a person
you are always telling you love,
do something that will
validate your love.

No failure is final, save our failure
to accept God's grace and forgiveness.

———

The compulsion to perfection
will destroy us if we don't recognize
and control it.

*R*elationships survive and grow as we
give to each other what we all need
for personal wholeness:
time, attention, interest—
in short, the human touch of love.

*T*here is nothing more healing
than to forgive
and be forgiven.

*T*he test is not whether
we are making a living
but whether
we are making a life.

*I*nstead of asking,
"Why is this happening to me?"
we need to ask, "What can I learn
from this experience?"

*P*reoccupation with self
limits our relationships.
If we are always wondering why
people act toward us the way they do,
we can't be free in responding to them.
Why did she do that?
What does he want now?
Why did he look at me that way?
Preoccupation with ourselves and our
situations will make us helpless.

*W*e can't help growing old,
but we don't have to become aged.
Becoming aged means
losing interest in life.

———

*T*here are ways for us to learn
without the risk of destruction.
Trust others who have been there.

I'm certain of three things:

1) I determine in large part
what I am becoming.

2) I do not have to be tomorrow
what I am today.

3) God not only has a dream
and a purpose for my life,
God provides the power
and guidance for my becoming.

We are responsible
not to the expectations of others,
but to the gifts God has given us.

*G*od does not allow temptation
in order to threaten our faith
but to deepen it.

*I*f we don't control our tongue,
every part of our life is threatened.

*L*ife is not something that
has to be won
nor something that has to be earned.
It's a gift to be enjoyed.

When we are loved,
we are made all over again.
When we love another,
we give them a new chance at life.

*I*f something is worth worrying about,
it is worth spending the energy
to change it.

One way to measure maturity
is to count the times we use
we rather than *I* in conversation.

We grow and become partners
in meaningful relationships,
not by forging a mold into which
others must fit but by the freedom
our love provides.

*L*ife is too important to wait
until we can get rid of our crutches
before we begin to live it.

We can sell our integrity for money.
We can sell our sense of self-worth
by doing those expected things to fit in.
We can sell our capacity to dream
by settling for security.
We can sell our character
by compromising our values.

*M*any of us defend our
failure to speak affirming words
by arguing that what we do
matters far more than what we say.
It isn't so.
Silence is a poor signal for love.

*I*t is only as we discover
how much life can hurt
that we are willing to share
the hurts of others.

*I*t is a great tragedy to die
without knowing who we are.
The greater tragedy is to live,
denying who we are.

We build our vocabulary
by claiming and using new words
until they are a part of our language.
It is also true with the
shaping of our character.
If we claim gentleness and practice it,
we will become gentle persons.
If we commit ourselves to truth,
we will become persons of integrity,
and folks will trust us. As the use
of words builds our language banks,
so the virtues we claim and practice
will build our lives.

*I*f we see ourselves as dogs,
we will find ourselves acting
like dogs—and dogs eat dogs.
But if we see ourselves a little less
than God, a little lower than the angels,
how we act and how we relate to others
will become God-like.

*L*iving depends on loving.

————

*T*here is a difference in
working with God and
working for God.

When we are suffering,
it doesn't help to compare ourselves
to others.

———

Love is decision
and
marriage is commitment.

We have roots in the past,
but we are not root-bound.
We salute the future,
but we do not pledge our
total allegiance to it.
This puts us mostly in the present,
where we really belong—
and where we can really be!

*L*ife isn't fair, but life isn't God.
God is good
and will someday
make up for all unfairness.

*I*f cursing the darkness means
condemning it, then we need to curse it
as well as light a candle.

We know what God is
going to do because we have seen
what God has done.

*H*onesty must be tempered by caring.
It's mean to be honest with someone
unless they know you really care
for their feelings.

———

*T*rouble comes when we
live beyond our means,
but what about living beyond
our meanings?

*W*e must free ourselves
from the blame of painful things
that happened from good intentions—
good intentions that may have been
applied improperly.

———

*M*any of us are dead
long before we are buried.

We can't cross the bridge to the future
until we have burned the bridge
to the past.